Rise and Be Healed

Receiving Healing and Deliverance

Chad MacDonald

Unless otherwise stated, all Scripture quotations are taken from the King James Version.

ISBN 978-1537246260

Copyright © 2017 by Chad MacDonald

Cover Design by John Polk

All Rights Reserved

Library of Congress Catalog Card Number: Pending

Printed in the United States of America

What Others Are Saying about 'Rise and Be Healed'

Dear Brother Chad,

It was an honor for me to read the manuscript of the new book you are writing.

As, you know we have travelled together, sharing the Glorious Gospel with thousands, and I have observed you before each service, on your knees in intercessory prayer... Sometimes for an hour or more, and you would come out for ministry with the power of God on you. And I thought, right there is the source of your ability through the Holy Spirit to cast out devils and heal sickness and diseases... Night after night I witnessed you with great authority naming the demons that held people bound and casting them out... It was very thrilling for me. And then to witness the great response of the people...

It makes me think of a certain Jew named Apollos – born in Alexandria, an eloquent man, and mighty in the scriptures, who came to Ephesus. Acts 18:25 makes me think of you: an eloquent man, and mighty in the scriptures 25 who was instructed in the way of the Lord; and being fervent in the spirit, he spake and taught diligently the things of the Lord...

I appreciate you, Brother Chad and the fire and the spirit of God in your life. The sacrifices you are making, being away from home and family in order to bring deliverance to the multitudes. I have never seen you step to the pulpit without being well prepared, always giving a mighty deliverance message. May your book "Rise and be Healed" be received by multitudes who are in need of healing and deliverance.

By embracing the truths of this book, any doubts and any spirit of unbelief will wash away.

More than just being filled with stories both true and often humorous, Rise and Be Healed should be considered a manual for both believer and unbeliever about the deliverance power of our Creator.

Your friend, Always,

Rev. Max Manning

Global Missions

Not a truer statement in all of history has been issued than when Walter Taylor penned the hymn "Calvary Covers It All." In Evangelist Chad MacDonald's book, he reminds us of our Sozo package from Christ, paid for by the shedding of His blood and the stripes on His back. Healing, deliverance, salvation, anything that we need for the abundant life, Jesus promised is ours, and this book points us to that great truth. You can experience your healing by reading the pages of this anointed book and allowing the same Spirit that raised Christ from the dead quicken your mortal body. Healing is the children's bread, and Brother Chad puts it in simple, relatable terms to encourage you to receive your healing today!

Pastor Roger Randel

Family of God Church, Topeka KS

From his own experience and the Word of God Chad MacDonald presents the premise that sin separates and the enemy seeks to bring sickness and destruction. He encourages us that Christ offers abundant life.

Read and be blessed. Use this tool as a help in your life and share it with those who need this message of hope and truth regarding healing and deliverance.

Dr. Billie Reagan Deck

Cedars of Lebanon, Inc.

TABLE OF CONTENTS

INTRODUCTION

At 10 years of age my uncle was buried beneath a pile of neighborhood friends. This time something was different. As he clutched the football and went down in the pile, something in his lower arm snapped and with it immense pain. When he finally emerged from the heap of bodies, fear gripped his heart as the pain coursed throughout his being. The only thought now consuming his young mind was to get his mother.

As he ran home with tears streaming down his face, he was now flanked by his two sisters who with great concern for their brother were equally frantic. The scene was now chaotic as they burst through the front door. Hearing the noise and commotion, my grandmother emerged from the kitchen and commanded my aunt and mother to be silent so that she could assess what was the matter.

There standing before her was her 10 year old son with a severe break in his lower arm. The bone could clearly be seen broken and protruding beneath the skin. For a young boy, the pain was unbearable as he stood there unable to move his arm.

My grandmother was Elsie Loraine Zombro and she was a woman full of faith and of the Holy Ghost. She was the greatest Christian I have ever met in my entire life.

A woman who raised 5 children practically alone in an era when there was no such thing as a government handout. All that my precious grandmother needed in life was Jesus; and that was enough for her.

That proved enough for her on the day my uncle broke his arm. In fact she took one look at his arm, and with the force of a giant grabbed it and began to speak in tongues. She fervently prayed, calling on the name of Jesus and as she did the very presence of God descended into that living room.

As my mother would later tell me concerning this event "We felt that if we moved off of that couch while mother prayed, the very hand of God would strike us down; we could sense such an awesome presence of the Lord fill the very room".

"In the name of Jesus Christ.." my grandmother shouted as she began to turn and open her sons limp arm; and as she did the very broken bone itself fused back together in place and the pain immediately disappeared. As if my grandmother expected no less; she looked at her children present in that room and announced; "Say thank you Jesus!" Having given the Lord some praise, she then turned and went right back into the kitchen while my uncle ran out the door totally healed by the power of God.

And wouldn't you know, that for a 10 year old, it meant right back out to the football game!

This story and testimony of the healing power of Jesus Christ has welded itself on the hearts and in the heritage of my family. This is the type of faith my grandmother walked in and this is the heritage of faith my beautiful grandmother both taught and imparted to me.

As a young child, one of the earliest scriptures I can ever recall her sharing with me was John 14:14 ***"If ye shall ask anything in my name, I will do it."***

She would often slide her worn bible over towards me and point to that exact spot. "What does that say?" She would ask; wanting me to see it for myself, knowing that she was planting seeds of faith deep inside my young heart.

That was the kind of woman she was.

She simply, like Abraham, believed God.

She believed the word of God and if God said it, that was good enough for her.

Oh how I miss that saint of God today. How I miss the way her face would light up when you would talk about Jesus. How I miss the way she would dance and praise the Lord in church and without warning, fall out under the power of the Holy Spirit without anyone even being near.

My grandmother 11 years ago left this planet and has been dancing in the streets of heaven ever since. It is to her I dedicate this work; and I pray that as you read this book, faith would come alive in your heart to believe God.

Whatever you may have heard, perhaps it's; 'No hope', perhaps its 'No cure', perhaps it's the blackened voice of damnation that tells you 'you'll never be free'. Maybe you've heard someone say that miracles don't happen anymore?

My prayer for you is that as you read this book you will understand that the same Jesus that walked the dusty streets of Jerusalem almost 2000 years ago has never changed.

He not only is still in the healing business, but he already made your healing a settled reality through the redemptive work of his cross.

"Jesus Christ the same yesterday, and today, and forever."

Hebrews 13:8

Chapter 1

The Origin of Sickness

When God created this planet along with our pristine parents Adam and Eve, the word of God declares:

"And God saw everything that He made and behold it was very good." (Genesis 1:31)

The world that God originally created was perfect. It was without pain and suffering. It was without sin, sickness or the corruption of Satan. So what happened?

It was one simple act of outright rebellion where God's prized creation in mankind sided with Satan. That one act of disobedience forfeited dominion and capitulated it from Adam to Satan. This opened the way for sin to corrupt all of creation.

As the result of that moment of disobedience mankind was banished from the Garden of Eden and forced into a now cruel and cold world. This was a world which was now crushed beneath the weight of a curse. A world that at one time knew no death or disease was now infected with sin and its stark consequences.

Sickness and disease is the result of sin.

Its origin can be traced back to the corrupting influence of Satan's overthrow of Adam's dominion in creation.

"Wherefore, as by one man sin entered into the world, and death by sin: and so death passed upon all men, for all have sinned."(Romans 5:12)

Death is but simply the matured process of sickness in its final form. If there would have been no sin in the world there would have subsequently been no sickness or death.

Sickness and disease exist in this world from the direct result of humanities fall from grace and the indirect influence of Satan in the earth.

However, many times satanic influence is directly involved in specific sicknesses or diseases.

"And ought not this woman, being a daughter of Abraham, whom Satan hath bound, lo, these eighteen years, be loosed from this bond on the Sabbath day?" (Luke 13:16)

Job also declares that his affliction was the direct result of the activity of Satan.

"So Satan went forth from the presence of the Lord, and smote Job with sore boils from the sole of his foot unto his crown."(Job 2:7)

The ministry of our Lord Jesus Christ was centered on liberating man from this demonic oppression.

"How God anointed Jesus of Nazareth with the Holy Ghost and with Power: who went about doing good, and healing all that were oppressed of the devil; for God was with him"(Acts 10:38)

Is all sickness a direct demonic attack? No.

However, all sickness is rooted in the satanic influence of this sin cursed world.

In either case our Lord Jesus Christ came to redeem us from sin, its effects and its curse.

"Christ hath redeemed us from the curse of the law, being made a   curse for us: for it is written, Cursed is every one that hangeth on a tree. (Galatians 3:13)

"The Spirit of the Lord is upon me, because he hath anointed me to preach the gospel to the poor; he heath sent me to heal the broken hearted, to preach deliverance to the captives, and recovering of sight to the blind, to set at liberty them that are bruised." (Luke 4:18)

Humanity clearly according to these scriptures was bound by Satan. The sinister arch enemy of God was behind it all holding God's prized creation in bondage.

But I have good news for you; Jesus came to set the captives free.

The bible is clear that Satan has only one agenda;

"The thief cometh not, but for to steal, and to kill, and to destroy." (John 10:10)

So what is it that is going on around you?

How can you discern its true origin?

Is it killing, stealing or destroying life?

If it is, then that is a clear red flag concerning its origin.

So let's finish the scripture because while Satan may be a destroyer, Jesus is a life giver.

"I am come that they may have life, and that they might have it more abundantly." (John 10:10)

The origin of the scourge of both disease and sickness is rooted in both the curse of sin and humanities bondage to Satan through that sin.

Since sickness is the result of the curse of sin. Sickness is actually a form of death to your body in the same manner sin is death to your spirit.

Sickness left alone in the body will do what sin left alone in the spirit will do.

Eventually it will kill you.

What the first Adam did through his rebellion however, is not greater than what the second Adam, The Lord Jesus Christ did on the cross.

One of the greatest schemes and tactics of the enemy is the lie that God does not heal any longer. This doctrine of devils has like leaven permeated the body of Christ.

"Tradition is the thief of power. There is no area of our lives where that theft is more evident than in the area of divine healing." Dr. Rod Parsley

As God sent His Son into the earth to heal our spiritual sickness which is sin, he also came to heal our physical bodies of sickness and disease.

We live in a world today that seems to be ravaged by sickness and disease.

Words like cancer, heart disease, stroke and diabetes seem to instantly paralyze society with fear.

If there has ever been a time when a fresh revelation of God's provision regarding divine healing and abundant life is necessary; today is that time.

The Holy Spirit is calling the body of Christ to arise from the ashes of powerlessness and the coals of complacency and begin to declare the whole council of God's word.

"My tears were wiped away, my heart was strong, I saw the way of healing...I said, "God help me now to preach the Word to all the dying around, and tell them how 'tis Satan still defiles, and Jesus still delivers, for He is just the same today." John Alexander Dowie

Chapter 2

Divine Healing and the Ministry of Jesus

There have been many so called preachers and theologians that have declared that the days of miracles and divine healing are over. Nothing could be further from the truth.

God has always been a healer, its part of his nature. He heals because it's His nature to heal.

In the Old Testament, when the children of Israel were in the wilderness the Lord issued a promise to his people. He declared that if the children of Israel would be diligent to obey the voice of the Lord he would be their healer.

" I am the LORD that healeth thee." Exodus 15:26

The Lord Jesus Christ, the Son of the Living God centered His ministry on earth around the miraculous. His ministry was about one thing and one thing only and that was to destroy the dominion and works of the devil.

"For this purpose the Son of God was manifested, that he might destroy the works of the devil." 1 John 3:8

In fact, Jesus centered His ministry around putting the devil out of business everywhere He went.

Wherever Jesus went he was bankrupting Satan's schemes. All across Judea and Israel the devil was frantically putting up proverbial 'out of business' signs all around as our Lord, the King of Glory manifested His power over Satan and his fallen kingdom by healing the sick, casting out of devils, raising the dead and preaching the gospel of the Kingdom of God.

"And Jesus went about all Galilee, teaching in their synagogues, and preaching the gospel of the kingdom, and healing all manner of sickness and all manner of disease among the people. And his fame went throughout all of Syria: and they brought unto him all sick people that were taken with divers diseases and torments, and those which were lunatic, and those that had the palsy; and he healed them." (Matthew 4:23,24)

"When the even was come, they brought unto him many that were possessed with devils: and he cast out spirits with his word, and healed all that were sick" (Matthew 8:16)

Notice what the scripture says in Matthew 8; "HE HEALED ALL. "

Jesus made healing the sick and diseased a major part of his ministry. In fact the preaching of divine healing was such a major part of his ministry that he instructed his disciples to proclaim that truth in every city they visited.

"And heal the sick that are therein and say unto them, The kingdom of God is come nigh unto you." Luke 10:9

"And as ye go, preach, saying, The kingdom of heaven is at hand. Heal the sick, cleanse the lepers, raise the dead, cast out devils: freely ye have received, freely give. "Matthew 10:8,9)

Everywhere the Lord went he not only demonstrated mastery over sickness and the devil but he commanded and ordained his disciples to do the same.

"Then he called his twelve disciples together, and gave them power and authority over all devils and to cure diseases. And he sent them to preach the kingdom of God and to heal the sick." (Luke 9:1,2)

Jesus came not only to save humanity from sin but to totally redeem mankind from the curse of the law. Part of the curse of sin is sickness and disease. The Lord Jesus Christ centered his ministry on setting the captives free from every level of bondage; from demons, depravity and disease.

Everywhere the Master went he opened the eyes of the blind, made crippled limbs straight, rebuked fevers, raised the dead and healed all manner of disease. Nothing was a match for the power of his word.

Jesus Christ himself is the living breathing word of Almighty God; at the power of his word sickness flees and disease disappears.

"He sent his word, and healed them." (Psalms 107:20)

John himself declared that revelation of truth when he announced in the gospel he penned so eloquently.

"In the beginning was the Word, and the Word was with God, and the Word was God. The same was in the beginning with God. All things were

made by him; and without him was not any thing made that was made." (John 1:1-3)

"And the Word was made flesh, and dwelt among us, and we beheld his glory, the glory as of the only begotten of the Father, full of grace and truth." (John 1:14)

Here the scripture plainly tells us that Jesus who is the Word of God Himself, put on a suit of flesh and became the literal fulfillment of Psalms 107:20.

"He sent His word, and healed them, and delivered them from their destructions."

Chapter 3

The Children's Bread

"But Jesus said unto her, Let the children first be filled: for it is not meet to take the children's bread, and to cast it unto the dogs."

(Mark 7:27)

This was a harsh statement to a woman who had just come to Jesus in an attempt ask him to heal her daughter. This Greek woman whose daughter was grievously possessed by an unclean spirit came begging the Lord for help.

However, Jesus literally responded to her and announced that she had no right to ask for such healing, since she was not Jewish. But did this stern rebuke deter a persistent, desperate and determined woman? No!

While she had no right-not being of the descended familial lineage of Abraham's seed, she knew she had no other choice but to cast herself on the mercy of the Son of God.

She humbled herself and declared:

"And she answered and said unto him, Yes Lord: yet the dogs under the table eat of the children's crumbs" (Mark 7:28)

As this desperate mother humbled herself to the Lordship of the Messiah her faith and persistence got the attention of the Great I AM Himself.

As Matthew's account records

"Then Jesus answered and said unto her, O woman, great is thy faith: be it unto thee even as thou wilt." (Matthew 15:28)

 The bible declares that immediately as the Lord spoke those words her daughter was instantly made whole.

This woman received her deliverance not based on what she deserved but on who Jesus was.

Let that thought sink in.

It is the nature of God to heal and deliver

Jesus is a healer. He is a deliver.

Healing and deliverance is the children's bread!

As a believer in the Lord Jesus Christ, healing belongs to you. Deliverance is your settled right.

It's part of the promise to all believers.

The scripture clearly declares:

"That the blessing of Abraham might come on the gentiles, through Jesus Christ" (Galatians 3:14)

What blessing?

The blessings and promises of the children of Abraham, every single one of them belong to you. Through faith in the Lord Jesus Christ we become sons of God and joint heirs with Christ. As an heir and child of the King you are entitled to eat at the Fathers table.

This bread of healing awaits all who will accept it.

It's your portion.

God made provision for your healing in the work of Jesus Christ on the cross.

Many wonder, does God still heal today?

The answer is a resounding YES!

Healing belongs to you.

It's your right, if you are a child of God, it is your bread. You are entitled to it. Jesus himself called it the children's bread. It's about time that you quit eating from the husks of the world and feeding on the lies of the enemy. It's time for you to pull yourself up to your Father's table and eat of the bread He has provided. The bread of deliverance!

In order to fully understand that healing belongs to every believer we have to fully understand what it is that Jesus did for us on the cross.

Healing is provided for all believers through the atonement of the blood of Jesus Christ.

The prophet Isaiah prophesied this when he announced:

"But he was wounded for our transgressions, he was bruised for our iniquities: the chastisement of our peace was upon him: and with his stripes we are healed." (Isaiah 53:5)

The Apostle Peter quotes this same prophecy when he declares

" by whose stripes ye were healed." (1 Peter 2:24)

I want you to look at something closely.

Isaiah declares: 'with his stripes we are healed' and Peter announces: 'by whose stripes ye were healed'.

As the foretelling prophet, Isaiah through a vision of the Holy Spirit saw the scourging, whipping and crucifixion of our Lord as it happened.

That is why he uses the term 'we are healed'.

Peter on the other hand however, is looking back at the event after it already occurred and declares: 'ye were healed'.

It is already a done deal.

Jesus paid it all on the cross.

He took those brutal stripes across his back for your healing.

It's yours!

Your healing was purchased through the blood of Jesus Christ and by the stripes he bore across his back.

Peter calls it a finished work.

Jesus Christ, the Lamb of God already healed you 2000 years ago. All you have to do is receive it.

There are many modern and so called theologians and preachers who try and explain this away.

They claim that the healing spoken of here was only spiritual healing and not physical healing.

Nothing could be further from the truth!

Let's let scripture interpret scripture and see exactly how this was fulfilled.

Look at what Matthew writes:

"When the even was come, they brought unto him many that were possessed with devils: and he cast out the spirits with his word, and healed all that were sick. That it might be fulfilled which was spoken by Isaias the prophet, saying Himself took our infirmities, and bare our sicknesses."(Matthew 8:16,17)

If that prophecy was only meant to include spiritual sin then why does Matthew quote it and write that the Lord was fulfilling it by healing the sick and casting out devils? The word of God is very clear here; Jesus not only suffered for your sin but suffered and shed his blood for your healing. In the Hebrew, the word for atonement is kaphar. That word literally means: to cover over, to be canceled, to pacify and make payment for. So when we say atonement and speak of the blood of Jesus Christ shed on the cross being that atonement; what are we saying?

We understand and are saying that the judgment of sin in its entirety was cancelled. All the curse of sin its consequences and sickness was cancelled out. The payment that was necessary to cover that charge was applied.

Your sickness and sin was completely 'atoned for' it was literally wiped out and paid for. In order to redeem mankind and restore humanity back to its original state before the fall, payment had to be rendered.

The only payment holy enough and perfect enough to cover such a putrid debt in its entirety once and for all, was the sinless blood of Jesus.

The spotless and perfect Lamb of God paid for your healing and covered your sins.

If God didn't want you healed, then he shouldn't have already healed you.

"Christ hath redeemed us from the curse of the law, being made a curse for us: for it is written, Cursed is every one that hangeth on a tree." (Galatians 3:13)

As the Son of God hung on that cross; bleeding and gasping for breath, as he suffered so greatly the punishment that was rightfully due us he lifted up his head and uttered three powerful words:

"It is finished". (John 19:30)

What a profoundly powerful statement.

Jesus paid it all. It is finished.

The payment for sin and its consequences had been completely rendered.

With those three words the remedy for your sickness and disease had been applied. It is a finished fact.

Nothing else need be done. It is complete and finalized.

Not one more drop of blood need be shed for you to be free. Not one more drop of blood need be shed for you to be forgiven. Not one more drop of his precious blood need be shed for you to be healed. Not one more drop of His blood need be shed for you to be delivered. Whatever it is your facing-sickness, cancer, disease, depression, despair or addiction. Jesus finished what he came to do. He set you free through the power of his cross. Understand that God is glorified through healing and deliverance not through sickness and suffering.

IT IS FINISHED.

Chapter 4

Is it God's will to heal me?

Faith can only exist where the will of God is known.

In order to really get a revelation of this truth and receive your healing we must understand what the will of God is.

It is impossible to have faith for something when the will of God is unsure.

First let's establish one thing: God did not put sickness on you to teach you a lesson.

I've heard such lies and foolish comments like that statement so many times. It is an ignorant statement and couldn't be farther from the truth.

It is absolutely the will of God for you to be healed.

There are thirty five major miracles listed in the gospel accounts which were performed by Jesus.

Not a single time did the Lord of Glory respond to a single person who came for healing by saying "I'm sorry I can't heal you today because I put that on you to teach you something."

It is the absolute will of God for you to be healed.

In fact if God did not want you healed, he shouldn't have already healed you.

In God's eyes he already purchased your healing.

In order to obtain it, you just need to receive it by faith.

Remember, *"by whose stripes ye were healed."* *(1 Peter 2:24)*

There are three questions asked in the gospel accounts regarding divine healing.

Let us take a look at these questions.

The first question occurred when Jesus came across a man riddled with a horrible disease called leprosy.

Mark's gospel records this account as the leper came to Jesus. In humility and with much begging he fell at the feet of the Lord and cried out.

"If thou will, thou can make me clean"

What was he saying to Jesus?

He was crying out: Lord if it's your will, you can heal me.

What was Jesus's response?

"I will; be thou clean." (Mark 1:41)

Jesus declared emphatically to him; it is my will!

He said "I will", not maybe, but I WILL.

Jesus didn't respond by asking the man if he was a good person.

He didn't ask if he knew all the books of the law. He didn't ask him a thing.

He simply just thundered to the leper- "I WILL"!

I have heard people utter that ageless demonic lie that says. "God put this on me to teach me something, it must be God's will."

Nothing is a more sinister fallacy than that statement! It is not only unscriptural but it is demonic to its core.

When asked if it was His will, Jesus responded with two words and forever settled the question. "I WILL!"

The second question came from a man who had a son that was severely bound by demonic power.

He had previously taken his son to the Lord's disciples but they seemingly could not cast the devil out. The man was so distraught and pleading for help that finally as a last resort he brought his boy to Jesus.

The father of the boy asked Jesus and said.. "if you can do anything please help us..."

Can you hear the desperation in this father's voice?

I love how Jesus responds to this distraught man who is down to his last resort.

Jesus said unto him:

"If thou canst believe, all things are possible to him that believeth." (Mark 9:23)

What was Jesus telling this man?

He was announcing to him; it is not a question of what I can do, only of what you can believe!

The true test of faith rests not in if you believe He can. Faith makes its abode in the truth that God 'WILL'. Every Christian knows God can, but few seem to know that He will.

One the most fatal mistakes made concerning divine healing and those seeking it, is the confusing of hope with faith. Sick people when prayed for will naturally hope they get better however, hope is not faith. Hope is passive by nature. It is most assuredly different from faith. Faith is active, creative and violent in nature. Hope clings to an element of uncertainty, looking only forward to possibility. Faith looks backwards to an accomplished fact. Faith has steady confidence and assurance resting solely on God's word. Faith needs no encouragement through visible means or faculties. Faith is not concerned with what it sees or feels. Faith draws its strength on the immutability of God's word. The assurance that God will do exactly what He said. That is why Jesus declared, *"All things are possible to him that believes.."*

What are you expecting God to do?

The third question came this time not from man to God, but from God to man. The bible declares that Jesus came upon a crippled man lying by the pool of Bethesda in John chapter 5.

The word of God tells us that this man was in this condition for 38 years. The average life span of an adult male in these times was only around 40 years old.

So here we see an individual who was bound by this infirmity for almost his entire known life. He was lying by the pool when Jesus approached him.

Jesus said to him:

"Wilt thou be made whole?"

Do you want to be healed Jesus asked him.

This is an important question that was asked directly from the lips of our Savior to this man.

Do you want to be healed?

Often many will never receive their miracle because they don't really want it.

They have assumed a victim mentality and revel in the attention their affliction brings them. They either enjoy the constant petting and attention their condition brings or have in some cases become reliant on the subsidies it brings them.

Disability payments are a major source of easy subsidies that some are not willing to relinquish. After all many have simply become comfortable in their mess.

Some individuals seem to even glory in their affliction.

You will find this in the chronic reveler.

This is the individual who when asked how they are doing, promptly spares no time in rattling off every one of their 52 aches and pains and the severity of each one.

They always seem to have to have it worse off than the person next to them.

This man had lain by the pool for 38 years, waiting for the stirring of the waters.

Can you imagine the disappointment and depression he might have felt as he watched those waters stir so many times before, unable to muster the strength or ability to get into that healing pool?

The utter frustration he must have experienced as he would lay there all alone while others were healed around him.

It seemed that he was on the outside looking in.

Have you ever been there?

It was always someone else that got their miracle, always the other person but never him.

Finally Jesus approached this man who had seemingly given up hope.

Do you want to be healed asked the Son of God?

With all of his years of waiting it seemed that his day for a miracle had finally arrived.

However his answer to the Lord was not a resounding yes.

His first response was "I have no man to carry me into the waters".

He was making excuses for himself.

He had allowed the victim mentality to take over his mindset.

Let me tell you one thing; YOU DON'T NEED A MAN!

All you need is Jesus; and this man didn't even realize who it was that was speaking to him.

He had experienced disappointment for so long he didn't even recognize God when he finally showed up.

So the third question is: Do you want to be healed?

Are you ready for your miracle?

It is unequivocally the will of God for you to be healed.

It is not enough to say that God is simply able to heal.

Everyone knows that.

The crux of faith rests not in the ability of God but in the will of God.

I am so tired of hearing statements like "If it's your will Lord".

That statement implies doubt and wavering.

There is no such thing as faith where the will of God is unsure.

It is absolutely the will of God to heal you; it's his nature to heal. He is the Healer.

As I said before, the battle of your faith is won or lost in the arena of your expectancy, what are you believing God to do?

"Beloved, I wish above all things that thou mayest prosper and be in health, even as thy soul prospereth." (3 John 1:2)

Here physical health is listed separately from the salvation of the soul. John writes through the inspiration of the Holy Ghost that it is his will that you be in health *in addition* to your soul prospering.

It is not the will of God that pain and disease rack your body.

Jesus came to heal you, healing is your right.

"God would rather have us doubt His ability than His willingness." F.F. Bosworth

Chapter 5

Activated by Faith

Now that we have established that it is in fact God's will to heal you.

How exactly does one receive their healing?

The first thing necessary to receive anything from God is faith.

Unbelief will always stifle a move of God.

We see this occur as Jesus returned to his hometown in Matthew's gospel.

"And he did not many mighty works there because of their unbelief". (Matthew 13:58)

Here we see the King of Glory; God himself walking the earth and the bible tells us that he was unable to perform miracles in a certain place.

What an amazing concept!

Surely he was able to do it-after all God is sovereign.

He by the word of his mouth spoke the heavens and the earth into existence. By the power of his word, light pierced the darkness and the stars were flung into their sockets.

So then how is it possible that he could not perform many mighty works in his home country?

Simply because of unbelief.

God will not impose himself on the will of mankind. He will not simply force himself on his creation, he desires fellowship.

He wants you to capitulate your heart to him and accept him.

He desires your acceptance.

In order to have this belief, this kind of faith, you must understand his will concerning your healing. It is his will.

God wants to heal you.

Regardless of what your past may be, what you may have done, or even if you think you don't deserve it.

Let me say this...that if we got what we deserved none of us would be alive!

Jesus Christ wants to heal you.

He is a loving God and grieves when you grieve. He sees your pain and suffering.

He desires that you reach out to him in faith.

Two blind men had heard Jesus was in town.

They frantically stumbled out into the street and made their way behind the entourage of our Lord. Desperate to gain the attention of the great physician they began to cry out;

"Son of David, have mercy on us". They continued to cry out until finally the Lord said to them; "Believe ye that I am able to do this? (Matthew 9:28)

The men emphatically responded "Yes Lord" and then came the resounding response from the Master.

"According to your faith be it unto you" (Matthew 9:29)

It was their faith that unlocked their miracle.

Often it is the misconception of what faith truly is that makes healing not only difficult to understand but impossible to appropriate. The Bible truth concerning healing is no less clear than its truth concerning salvation. It is the understanding of the parallel for the faith required for either salvation and healing that holds the key to this truth. The healing of the body and salvation of the soul both involve the same working of the Spirit of God. It is faith in the finished work of Calvary's cross and the shed blood of Christ that has the power to obtain salvation. If the sinner does not have such faith and will not believe in the power of the finished work of Jesus Christ to save him, he will not be saved. If the sinner will not believe until he feels 'saved'-he will never be 'saved'. Such is the same for faith required for healing.

Let's take a look at the woman in Mark chapter 5.

The bible tells us that she had a severe issue of blood which had plagued her for 12 years.

In fact, it was believed to have been a serious venereal disease. This woman was considered unclean and forbidden to even be out in public. And because she was considered unclean, she was also rejected and ostracized.

Because she was rejected she was thus unwanted.

She had suffered and spent all her savings on the modern medical science of her day, but to no avail. (Mark 5:25-34)

Maybe you find yourself in the same predicament as this woman?

Perhaps you feel rejected and unwanted, unclean and unable to be free?

Perhaps modern medicine has given up on you?

Perhaps the diagnosis has hit you like a ton of bricks.

No hope, no help, no cure.

This woman faced that same sentence of death but refused to accept it. Something remarkable happened.

We are told that somehow she heard of Jesus.

"When she heard of Jesus" (Mark 5:27)

I don't know what it is she heard exactly, the scriptures don't tell us. Perhaps she had heard how Jesus raised the widow of Nain's son from the dead? Maybe she heard how he cleansed the leper or made crooked limbs to go straight? Perhaps she heard about blinded eyes popping open or fevers immediately fleeing his presence at the mention of his word? I don't know what she heard, but whatever it was it activated her faith deep inside her spirit.

She knew that all she had to do was get to Jesus.

It was what she heard about Jesus that sparked faith within her.

There is something special that happens when the gospel is preached by an anointed fivefold ministry office gift (Apostle, Prophet, Evangelist, Pastor or Teacher).

"How shall they call on him in whom they have not believed? And how shall they believe in him of whom they have not heard? And how shall they hear without a preacher?" (Romans 10:14)

It is the power of anointed preaching that God uses to stir faith. It is important that you get yourself under the ministry and preaching of a man or woman of God that believes in the whole counsel of God's word. A ministry that preaches Jesus is still healer, savior and deliverer. A ministry that believes it is God's will to heal you. (I'll cover this more a little later in the book)

So we do not know exactly what she heard, but whatever it was, her faith came alive.

She said to herself 'all I need to do is get to Jesus.' Her faith was so activated that she said,

"If I may touch but his clothes, I shall be whole" (Mark 5:28)

Her faith was so alive that she knew the verifiable power and glory of God resided in Jesus to the point that all she needed to do was reach out and grab ahold of the fringes of his garment. In desperation she did just that.

Faith has arisen in her and determination finally had ahold of her. She had refused to be refused and denied to be denied. She was going to get her miracle.

She finally made her way through the crowd and with the tenacity of a pit bull grabbed ahold of his garment in faith.

Immediately she was healed.

Jesus instantly felt healing power flow out of him as he then turned around in the massive throng.

He asked "Who touched me?"

Suddenly the frail woman emerged through the crowd and confessed; "it was me Lord".

What did Jesus say to her?

"Daughter, thy faith hath made thee whole" (Mark 5:34)

Her faith had healed her.

She did not go to Jesus thinking in her mind; "maybe I'll be healed, maybe if it's his will, if he's in a good mood" No not at all!

She said all I need to do is get to Jesus and touch his clothes and **"I shall be whole" (Mark 5:28)**

Not a maybe, but 'I shall be'.

This was an I know I don't see it yet, but I shall be!

Faith always says; I may not see it yet-but I shall be.

I want you to understand something.

God is not going to ruin his track record for you.

I know you may be thinking that you know someone who it didn't work for, but when faith is activated, reason is never required.

As I said, you must never forget. It is the battle of your faith that is won or lost in the arena of your expectancy.

So my question then to you is, what are you expecting God to do?"

We must understand that God is not moved by your need but rather it is your faith that moves the hand of God.

Your need may move the compassionate heart of the Master but it is your faith alone that will move His hand.

God will meet you at your point of need with his supply only once you have determined to stand firm on His word and believe that he will do just what he said he would do.

Faith in God does not require a plan B.

"God is not a man, that he should lie; neither the son of man, that he should repent; hath he said, and shall he not do it? Or hath he spoken, and shall he not make it good?" (Numbers 23:19)

Stand in faith on his word and know that if God said it you can take it to the bank!

The Roman centurion came to Jesus begging that he heal his servant. The centurion's servant was home on his death bed grievously ill. As the Roman soldier asked Jesus to come and heal him, the Lord responded simply:

"I will come and heal him". (Matthew 8:7)

Here we see the willingness of Jesus to immediately heal again.

I will come and heal him he declares!

The story however doesn't end there. The centurion stops him in his tracks and tells Jesus that he is not worthy that he should step under his roof. He tells Jesus that he understands authority and that when he commands a servant to do something he does it.

With the words only faith can muster, the Roman soldier declares to Jesus*; "speak the word only, and my servant shall be healed" Matthew 8:8)*

He didn't need Jesus to travel to his home. He understood this was God himself he was staring in the face. He understood that all Jesus needed to do was utter the command and it would be done. This man understood the power of the word of God.

This got the attention of Jesus as he marveled at this great display of faith.

"Verily I say unto you, I have not found so great faith, no, not in Israel." "Go thy way; and as thou has believed, so be it done unto thee." (Matthew 8:10,13)

Here we see it again; as you have believed so be it done to you.

This man received his answer based on the level of his faith.

Often one can receive their healing through immersing themselves in the word of God.

Through meditation on the scriptures concerning the promise of healing and God's remedy for their situation, faith suddenly begins to come alive.

It is then that they begin to declare and stand on those promises.

Remember the woman with the issue of blood? She said "I shall be made whole". It was not enough just to believe but she began to speak it. I can imagine as she frantically made her way towards Jesus, as faith was rising in her heart she began to say over and over 'I shall be', 'I shall be'.

"For verily I say unto you, That whosoever shall say unto this mountain, Be thou removed, and be thou cast into the sea; and shall not doubt in his heart, but shall believe that those things which he saith shall come to pass, he shall have whatsoever he saith." Mark 11:23

Let faith rise on the inside of you even right now to believe that you shall be made whole.

"Surely he hath borne our griefs, and carried our sorrows" Isaiah 53:4

The Hebrew word here for griefs is choli. This word actually means illness and sickness. The word for sorrows in Hebrew is makobah it is translated as pain and suffering. Jesus Christ the Lamb of God carried your sicknesses, pain and suffering across his back all the way up Golgotha's hill. But the most important word in this verse is the first one: "Surely".

Without a doubt, no question about it! "Surely"

"Surely" (It's a done deal) Jesus bore your sickness, disease, illness, pain and suffering.

He paid for your healing with the blood of his cross; receive it now by faith!

"Christians need never be sick, any more than they need to be sinful. It is always God's desire to heal you." T. L. Osborn

Chapter 6

The Healing Anointing

"And heal the sick that are therein and say unto them, The kingdom of God is come nigh unto you." (Luke 10:9)

I had been asked to come and preach the gospel at a rally located in a community park one afternoon. At that time I was still a student at World Harvest Bible College, now called Valor Christian College. I had been home on break when asked to come and preach this event.

As I finished my message and I gave the altar call, I noticed a young boy in a wheel chair to the right of the platform. He was grievously afflicted with the palsy and there surrounded by his family was bound by that wheel chair.

 I walked over to that young man and laid my hands upon him:

"In the name of Jesus Christ of Nazareth I command you, rise up and walk!"

The anointing of God hit me as I grabbed that 13 year old boy, lifted him up out of that chair and watched as he walked across the platform without his leg braces.

This young man had been in that chair since about the age of 2 years old, but by the power of God was healed and walked across that platform.

Glory to God!

Every devil in hell whispered, "You can't pray for a boy in a condition like that. Your still in Bible College, what if he doesn't walk, what if, what if?"

But I refused to listen to those thoughts and operated in faith.

I grabbed him and pulled him out of that chair commanding his healing in the name of Jesus, and he was healed by the miracle working power of God.

That was the first major miracle and healing that I ever saw God perform through my ministry. That was some 15 years ago and since then numerous people have been healed and delivered by the power of Jesus Christ.

"And these signs shall follow them that believe: they shall lay hands on the sick, and they shall recover" (Mark 16:17-18)

When Jesus walked the earth he empowered his disciples and commanded that they go into the cities and heal the sick, cast out devils, raise the dead and preach the gospel of the kingdom.

Nothing has changed since then. You cannot separate healing from the message of the gospel anymore than you could separate the forgiveness of sins from the gospel message.

The commission he gave to the disciples became the great commission.

Mark chapter16 bears this out, as just before his accession he gathered the disciples around and issued his last instructions. (Mark 16:15-18).

In fact our Lord commanded them to tarry in the city of Jerusalem until they be endued with power from on high. (Luke 24:49)

"But ye shall receive power, after that the Holy Ghost is come upon you" (Acts 1:8)

God never intended his church to be anything other than a replica of the entire book of Acts. He told his disciples to wait until they received the power of the Holy Ghost and were filled with the Spirit of God.

In fact, in other words he said- don't even think about going out to minister without it.

We live in an age when the church needs to get back to basics, back to the bible. Without power, preaching is simply story telling. Without power the gospel amounts to only another religious philosophy.

While much of the church has begun to embrace the modernistic theology that says miracles were only for the early church- they claim healings were only to jump start the church into the first century. With the world dying all around, people are in such bondage to demons, depravity and disease.

The church has instead become a dead cold sect in many places.

"Having a form of godliness but denying the power thereof" (2 Timothy 3:5)

The church is called to be the conduit for which the power of God flows through to change the world.

Sometimes an individual has tried over and over to receive healing or deliverance on their own but to seemingly no avail.

While often the individual can receive completely on their own as they stand firm on the word of God in declaration and faith. However, many times their healing and deliverance will only come through the ministry of the laying on of hands and through contact with the tangible anointing of God.

Jesus gave his disciples power over all devils and to cure diseases.

He them sent them out and commanded them to lay their hands on the sick. This is recorded all throughout the New Testament. (Luke 9:1,2) (Mark 6:12,13)

Any believer that is filled with the Holy Spirit can lay hands on the sick. (keyword is 'believer').

However there is something powerful about a fivefold ministry office gift that is full of the Holy Ghost and faith. A man or woman of God- called and anointed with the Holy Ghost and power, one who is **operating in** the gifts of the Holy Ghost.

Often this is necessary to destroy the yoke of sickness or demon power in the life of the individual.

"And the yoke shall be destroyed because of the anointing" (Isaiah 10:27)

The anointing of God was so strong and powerful in the life of Peter that they brought people out and lined the streets with the diseased and demon possessed so that just his shadow might pass by and they would be healed. (Acts 5:15,16)

Throughout the book of Acts- the sick, the diseased, the crippled and the afflicted were healed by the power of the Holy Ghost.

"And God wrought special miracles by the hands of Paul. So that from his body were brought unto the sick handkerchiefs or aprons, and the diseases departed from them, and the evil spirits went out of them." (Acts 19:11,12)

One of the nine wonderful gifts of the Holy Spirit given to those who have received the baptism in the Holy Ghost is the gifts of healing. The gift of the working of miracles is another.

"To another the gifts of healing by the same Spirit; To another the working of miracles" 1 Corinthians 12:9,10)

That is why I mentioned previously of the importance that the believer find a good Spirit filled church where the Lord is confirming his word with signs following.

Find a good church where the man or woman of God is full of the Holy Ghost and faith and where the gifts of the Holy Spirit are in operation in their life.

It's in an environment like this where you can begin to, as Dr. Lester Sumrall used to say "Feed your faith and starve your doubts to death"

God still uses the ministry of laying on of hands to effect healing.

"Is any sick among you? Let him call for the elders of the church; and let them pray over him, anointing him with oil in the name of the Lord: And the prayer of faith shall save the sick." (James 5:14,15)

The laying on of hands is a point of contact, a conduit. The anointing is tangible and can be transferred. When the man of God is laying hands on the sick, He is standing in the position of authority that was given to him by the Lord himself.

He places his or her hands on the individual in faith as a point of contact and the power of God will flow into the individual in need.

I was preaching during a crusade in Haiti and so many had flooded the altar seeking prayer for healing and deliverance that I could not go down the line and pray in the conventional manner as you would normally see in many churches. So I announced for the people to get in a single file line and come one after the other. I began to declare to the people while under the anointing of God, "I am the man of God and the anointing is present right here where I stand, Whatever it is that you need, when you come, come in faith. It is not necessary to tell me what it is you need, you just come and as you come I will lay my hand on your head and say 'In the name of Jesus', and as I do you receive whatever it is you need by faith. As you walk away begin to do something you couldn't do before..."

As they came the power of God fell upon them and so many were healed and delivered from demon power.

It is important however, that as you come forward in faith that you keep your faith directed toward Jesus and not man.

Jesus is the healer, not the man of God.

Chapter 7

Hindered Healing-Unbelief In The Pulpit

"Then Peter said, Silver and Gold have I none; but such as I have give I thee: In the name of Jesus Christ of Nazareth rise up and walk" (Acts 3:6)

I heard the story once of a young preacher who was invited to the Vatican by the Pope. He was taken inside the Vatican deposits and archives where few had ever been authorized to venture. As the young preacher was shown all of the gold and spoils that centuries had accumulated, in a prideful sense of accomplishment the Pope turned and announced "No longer need the church say silver and gold have I none any longer."

To which the young preacher promptly responded back

"And also no longer can she say rise up and walk."

What an indictment of many pulpits today!

Jesus intended his church to be a church of power and dominion.

In fact he pulled his disciples together and then imparted to them authority to do what he did.

"Then he called his twelve disciples together and gave them power and authority over all devils and to cure diseases." (Luke 9:1)

Either we believe the word of God or not.

Jesus said I give you authority over ALL devils AND to cure diseases.

Do we really believe that?

Do most of the pulpits really believe that today?

One thing is certain. You cannot give what you do not have.

Jesus made a profound statement to his disciples. He gathered them around and declared:

"Verily, verily I say unto you, He that believeth on me, the works that I do shall he do also; and greater works than these shall he do; because I go to my Father." (John 14:12)

He said those that believed on him would do greater works. What a truly profound announcement he made.

Just after our Lord rose from the dead and just prior to his ascension he made another statement.

Actually, it was a commandment.

He had just given his disciples the great commission and told them to go into all the world but just as soon as he commissioned them he quickly threw the brakes on them.

He commanded that they go nowhere until they had received the promise of the Father.

They were commanded in (Acts 1:4) not to go anywhere until they had received this promise. What was this promise?

"But ye shall receive power after that the Holy Ghost is come upon you." (Acts1:8)

Until his disciples had received the Holy Ghost and been endued with power they were considered useless. The infilling of the Holy Ghost was and still is a requirement for service.

Many in the modern 'Pentecostal or Spirit Filled' church get caught up on tongues. While I believe that speaking in tongues is part of the initial physical evidence of the Baptism in the Holy Ghost, the real evidence is the power for service we are to receive.

Jesus said we would receive explosive and dynamite power.

He said we would do greater works than even He, because He was going to send the 'Comforter' the Holy Spirit to any believer that asked for it.

Many times I have seen healing and deliverance fail to occur simply because the minister doing the 'praying or laying on of hands' isn't even convinced God will do it.

Individuals come forward for healing and then instead of finding a man of God full of faith and the Holy Ghost, they find a powerless puppeteer who doesn't expect God to miraculously move any more than the atheist down the street.

When the minister uses words like "Lord if it's your will", you need to run!

The man of God above all people should know God's will.

He shouldn't waiver in this question.

It is God's will to heal and set you free!

When the man or woman of God prays for the sick, it should be done from a position of authority.

They should be commanding the sick to be healed in the name of Jesus. They should be full of the Holy Ghost!

Remember the words of Peter, "Such as I have, give I thee".

You can't give what you don't have.

I've heard preachers make statements like- "There's nothing in my hands, no power here, these are just hands"

Well, if there is nothing in your hands Mr. Preacher, don't put them on me.

I have power inside of me-Holy Ghost power resides in my hands. My body is the temple of the Holy Ghost who dwells inside of me.

"Greater is He that is in me than he that is in the world"1 John 4:4

Chapter 8

Deliverance To The Captives

"The Spirit of the Lord is upon me, because He hath anointed me-to preach deliverance to the captives" Luke 4:18

My phone rang and I answered promptly. The voice on the other end was distraught. "Could I pray" she asked?

I was informed that a family member of this individual had just overdosed on Heroin and was being rushed to the emergency room.

I responded assuredly that I would go in person and lay hands on the boy. I raced to the local hospital and got there almost at the same time that the doctor was delivering the grim news to the family that now packed the consultation room to max capacity.

Screams and wailing echoed down the hall and the mother screamed "No!. Not my boy!"

Her boy was brain dead and had died instantly. It was too late!

Sorrow filled every heart as this young man was no more and grief filled the family.

Unfortunately this scene plays out all too familiar in hospitals across this nation.

The demonic scourge of drug addiction seemingly has a strangle hold on multiplied millions.

Something must be done! Something has to be done!

The church unfortunately has not been fulfilling its God given mandate. The modern church for the most part has been relegated to a giant referral service.

What the church used to cast out, we now try to counsel out.

We now refer alcoholics to AA and addicts to rehab. The church seems in many cases to be powerless to effect change in the lives of the hurting.

The most disturbing part of the entire story of the young man above is the fact that twice was he referred to and completed 'Teen Challenge'. Twice, a church referred him out rather than setting him free.

This young man wanted to be free. He tried living free from drugs, but the demons seemed to always keep calling. He would go for a short while and be clean only to relapse and fall again.

Over and over this diabolical cycle was repeated until finally it destroyed him.

This young man needed deliverance from devils of addiction. He did not need rehab.

He needed the delivering power of the Lord Jesus Christ!

He needed the church to be the church and be full of Holy Ghost power and set him free.

The real indictment lies in this story with the church that kept sending him out to complete a program that only deals with the superficial element and not the root.

When you want to get rid of a weed and you only cut the top, it will always grow back. You have to pull it up by the root!

Many who are struggling with drug addiction are bound by unclean spirits of addiction. They need to be cast out.

It's time that the church recognizes this truth and starts addressing it or more mothers will be grieving their children at the hands of a powerless pulpit.

I was preaching under a heavy anointing of God as a man stumbled into the service. He was physically under the influence of alcohol as he staggered to his seat.

This church was in a store front location and was connected literally to a bar next door.

But the devil made a drastic mistake that night and sent him to the wrong address!

I walked over to the gentleman and asked him "What can the Lord do for you?"

With tears in his eyes he looked at me and said "I want to be free from drugs and alcohol."

"Stand-up" I responded and informed him to lift his hands up.

"In the name of Jesus Christ, I command you foul devil of addiction..come out of him"

As I declared those words to him the power of God literally hit that man and threw him back into his seat and he began to shake under the mighty power of the Holy Spirit.

In an instant he not only was free but was completely sober.

Drug addiction is a devil and it bows the knee to the name of Jesus Christ!

Rehab centers exist in the void of a powerless Pentecost.

 Jesus said you would receive power after that the Holy Ghost has come upon you.

Power over addiction-Power over sickness-Power over devils

When an addiction is present and it presents a compelling and overwhelming control over an individual, deliverance is necessary.

If this young man suffering from such bondage could have been in contact with a man of God full of the anointing of the Holy Ghost and faith he could have been set free! Sadly, many churches not only do not preach deliverance but wouldn't know a devil if it stared them in the face.

Instead, he heard a self-help gospel message from a Pastor who was most likely afraid of scaring off funds for the offering plate by preaching on deliverance from demon power. Most likely this powerless preacher didn't even believe in or preach deliverance.

Jesus made deliverance from demon power a major theme and focus of his ministry.

Jesus had a deliverance ministry.

He delivered people from tormenting spirits which had ravaged and demonized the people and then he commanded his church to do the same.

Listen to the commandment of our Lord just before He ascended to the right hand of the Father.

"And these signs shall follow them that believe; In my name they shall cast out devils; they shall speak with new tongues; they shall take up serpents; and if they drink any deadly thing, it shall not hurt them; they shall lay hands on the sick, and they shall recover." Mark 16:17,18

Notice that the first sign that is to follow believers is that they would cast out devils. It does not say council them out, the word of God declares that they shall cast them out!

Much of addiction, sickness, disease and even sexual perversion is a direct result of demonic affliction. Notice in the scriptures that at times Jesus simply rebuked a fever or healed a sickness. In many other instances He however confronted the unclean spirits causing the affliction.

In Mark 9:25 we see Jesus address the demonic activity causing deafness and dumbness. *"Thou dumb and deaf spirit, I charge thee, come out of him, and enter no more into him."*

In this particular instance we observe that the boy's deafness and mute speech was the result of demonization.

In Matthew 9:33 we read:

"And when the devil was cast out the dumb spake: and the multitudes marveled, saying, It was never so seen in Israel"

Often times before the healing can take place, deliverance must come first. In this case it wasn't until the devil came out that the mute man was able to speak.

In the thirteenth chapter of Luke we read of a woman who was brutally afflicted with an extreme condition. The scriptures tell us that her back was so bowed down that she was literally stuck face down staring at her feet. For eighteen years she suffered like this-bound by extreme pain and discomfort. She was a living and breathing hunchback of the most severe case.

The Lord of Glory while standing before her recognized that something more sinister was at work here.

"And behold, there was a woman which had a spirit of infirmity eighteen years, and was bowed together, and could in no wise lift up herself." Luke 13:11

Her condition was the result of an unclean spirit. The Lord Jesus Christ wasted no time in addressing this foul being.

"And when Jesus saw her, he called her to him, and said unto her, Woman thou art loosed from thine infirmity."

A message came across my phone. It was a friend and colleague of mine in India. One of his young girls from his orphanage was gravely ill. He had become distressed and worried. She was not able to awake for days and would not eat.

Franticly searching for help they took her to the hospital but they could offer no such assistance. This young girl needed a miracle.

My friend messaged me his concern and as he began to tell me of her condition, the Holy Spirit spoke to me and told me the little girl was suffering from a demon.

I relayed what the Lord had told me and instructed him to stand over her, rebuke the devil and command it to come out of her in the name of Jesus.

Almost as fast as I sent the message came back his reply.

"Will you do it-I will call you"

In a few moments my friend was calling and placed me on speaker phone in the room where the girl was laying.

I began to pray and as I did the Holy Ghost came upon me. I rebuked those foul spirits of infirmity and death attempting to destroy that girl in the name of the Lord Jesus Christ. I commanded that they come out of her and that she be made whole instantly.

As soon as I finished praying she spoke up as I heard her declare, "Thank You."

She was instantly set free by the power of God.

I want to you to notice in Mark 16:18 where the word of God declares,

"They shall take up serpents"

The first thing I must address is that this is not speaking of that foolishness known as snake handling.

Often the best interpreter for scripture is scripture. The word of God is referring to the work of demonic spirits and demonic strongholds at work in this text.

Let's examine what Luke's gospel has to say.

"And he said unto them, I beheld Satan as lightning fall from heaven. Behold, I give unto you power to tread on serpents and scorpions, and over all the power of the enemy: and nothing shall by any means hurt you." Luke 10:18,19

Specifically here Jesus is referring to Satan and demonic power when he mentions serpents and scorpions. He gave his disciples power and authority over all power of the enemy. These unclean devils are the serpents spoken of here and in Mark chapter 16.

Now having addressed that, I want to draw your attention to the word 'take' in Mark 16:18.

"They shall take up serpents"

The Greek word for take in this instance is 'Airo'. It literally means to destroy, to formally remove, to cause to no longer experience.

Jesus is declaring here that one of the signs which shall follow His believers is the fact that they shall 'Airo' serpents. They shall forcibly destroy and remove demonic activity and strongholds in the life of people.

In His name, the name of the Lord Jesus Christ we have the authority to set people free from demonic strongholds.

This is the power to set them free as if they had never previously experienced such bondage.

Jesus came to preach deliverance to the captives!

I am not sure what may have you in bondage?

Perhaps it's an addiction to pornography, perhaps it's an addiction to drugs and alcohol, perhaps it's homosexuality, perhaps it's a debilitating disease or affliction? Maybe, its depression or tormenting thoughts of suicide, perhaps its night terrors?

Whatever it may be, you can be set free in the name of Jesus Christ. There is hope for you! Deliverance is the children's bread- it belongs to you.

Jesus paid for it with His precious blood on that cruel and splintering cross of Calvary.

Another demonic bondage prevalent and not properly addressed is a spirit of sexual immorality. Often it is present as a spirit of lust or pornography, adultery or homosexuality. Sexual bondage and perversion can be a very severe stronghold and in many cases if not most cases must be cast out.

Those who seemingly cannot be free or stay free from these compelling urges only to return like a dog to their vomit over and over again, must be set free.

I was contacted by an individual who had asked me for prayer. He announced "I am called to ministry but I am bound by pornography..will you pray for me?"

I asked this poor man "How long have you been bound?"

"For 50 years.." Came his shocking response.

"How old are you?" I asked

"I am 55" He replied.

This man went on to disclose how he was first exposed to this demonic stronghold at the age of 5 by a family member.

This man was bound by spirits of lust and perversion which tormented him daily.

He would seemingly do well for a while but eventually would always fall to these demonic and overwhelming urges.

This man's stronghold was almost as old as he was alive. He needed deliverance.

We must never shy away from addressing demonic activity and be content with a head in the sand mentality of naivety.

Wake up church!

Multitudes depend on our ability preach deliverance to the captives.

Chapter 9

Medicated Mindset

A recent Pew Research poll determined that in 2012, the pharmaceutical industry spent more than $27 billion on drug promotion and advertising. With more than $24 billion directed directly to physicians and $3 billion towards advertising mainly through television.

The pharmaceutical conglomerate based on this poll spends more the national GDP of 103 nations.

And most of it is targeted directly towards your healthcare professionals.

No wonder we live in a nation where they propagate a pill for everything.

We are being conditioned that there is a 'pill' for everything.

There is much more revenue to be made in developing medication and 'continuing treatment' than in there could ever be in finding an actual cure.

Because of this, we live in an environment that is highly overmedicated.

As the result of this mindset, it seems that many do not need God.

It seems that so many are content to 'just pop a pill'.

It has been asked before, "Why does it seem that God only heals and performs miracles mostly overseas and on the mission field?"

First let me say that God is no respecter of persons and He is unequivocally the same Lord in Africa as He is in America.

God's ability to heal is not bound by geographical distance but rather by your ability to believe.

The stark difference often lies in the ability of the people in these 'other' nations to believe in the supernatural miracle working power of God.

The people in these nations often are surrounded by the supernatural.

They know what it's like to see demonic power displayed through a voodoo priest or witch-doctor. They understand the supernatural realm and so they often find it easier to believe in the supreme and sovereign power of Jesus Christ after having finally heard the gospel.

They have not been subjected to the damnable modernistic atheistic doctrine of humanism.

Many times when the people in these impoverished nations are afflicted with sickness or disease they do not have the luxury of 'popping a pill' as we do here in the United States.

They have little to no access whatsoever to modern medical treatment and therefore have no other choice but to believe God for healing.

And God does not disappoint their faith!

Many times, the miracle working power of God to heal is hindered here in the United States simply because we have placed more faith in our prescription pills and medical professionals than the redemptive power of the blood of Christ. This ought not be!

I often say, In America we trust in the great prescription and in Africa they trust the Great Physician. I am however by no means teaching against modern medical treatment.

I am simply telling you, *"That your faith should not stand in the wisdom of men, but in the power of God." 1 Cor 2:5*

Chapter 10

The God of The Miraculous

When one of my sons was about a year old he loved to crawl behind our dog laughing hysterically as the dog would chase the cat around the house.

One morning the dog took off roaring through the house after the family cat. As the dog barreled underneath an end table after the cat, Michael was in hot pursuit.

There was a hot-potpourri oil container sitting on top of the table. The dog tore underneath it after the cat and knocked the entire container of oil across the bare back and arms of my one year old boy.

Instantly the flesh melted off of my boy's arms and back.

He screamed in agony as the oil seared into his flesh. In a panic, I rushed over and scooped my boy up and held him in my arms. His skin had completely dissolved across his entire back.

He was in severe pain and agony, but I could do nothing except pray.

As he writhed in intense misery, I began to call upon the name of Jesus loudly.

I agonized and travailed intensely, praying in the Holy Spirit. As I prayed over him and rebuked his pain and burnt flesh, I could feel the anointing of God suddenly come upon him.

I could see a literal grey cloud begin to lift off of him as he suddenly ceased to cry and calmed down.

The Lord touched my son that morning.

To this day my son does not have a single scar or trace of ever having been burned by the hot oil that day.

 There in my living room he was gloriously healed and made whole in the name of Jesus Christ.

Betty Baxter was born with all of the vertebrae in her back crushed. By the time she was 11 years old her back was completely bowed forward and her face was fused in a downward position. Living in intense pain and with her face literally stuck sideways against her knees she was bed ridden. Her heart was enlarged and the Doctors were powerless to help her. After traveling from doctor to doctor she was finally sent home to die.

The church Betty's family attended did not believe that God still healed today. They taught that damnable lie that says miracles were only for the early church.

Betty was without hope or help. Racked with pain she begged to die so she could finally be with Jesus and be free from torment.

But Betty's mother had been reading the word of God to her faithfully every day. One day she came across Hebrews 13:8. That scripture began to birth something on the inside of her as it thundered truth.

It read, *"Jesus Christ the same yesterday, today and forever"*.

If Jesus healed in the New Testament, Betty's mother thought surely he would still do it. Hope and faith began to rise inside her heart as she encouraged her hurting daughter with this new revelation. She was now convinced that this same Jesus would still heal her crippled daughter.

As Betty laid twisted and deformed in her room, suddenly a bright light appeared at the foot of her bed. Out of the glorious brightness of that light stepped the King of King's in all of His glory.

Standing at the foot of her bed, Betty recognized her Savior as Jesus reached His nail pierced hand towards her. In an instant, the nail scarred hand of the Lord of Glory touched her and like the force of a million electric volts the power of God coursed through her body. Immediately bones began to pop back into place. Her arms were beginning to twist back into position, her neck snapped back into proper alignment as the cracking of bone began to erupt all over her body. The knots that once covered her spine dissolved at the touch of the Masters hand. In a moment this young 11 year old girl jumped from her bed completely made whole and healed by the power of Jesus Christ.

My oldest boy was rushed to the hospital after having trouble breathing.

As I finally made my way to the emergency room there was my son, sitting on a hospital bed hooked up to oxygen.

The doctor was insistent on telling me that he had asthma and had admitted him to Womack Army Medical Center.

I wasn't about to accept that!

God was going to have the final say.

I walked into my son's room as he laid on the bed with IV's and mask hooked up to him.

My little 1 year old looked up at his daddy and I began to pray and forcibly command healing into his body. As I prayed the power of God touched my son and I began to immediately unhook his IV's and equipment.

"We are leaving.." I announced, as I picked him up and walked down the hall. Only to be chased down by a doctor who attempted to inform me what I couldn't do.

"You can't take him out of here like that.."

I informed the doctor that my boy was healed and we were going home whether he liked it or not.

They tried to tell me that he would have these so called 'asthma' problems for his entire life. Well, let me tell you something.

Chris is now 19 years old and has never had an attack or breathing problem ever since. He was and is completely healed by the power of God.

"And God said unto Moses, I AM THAT I AM: and he said, Thus shalt thou say unto the children of Israel, I AM hath sent me unto you."

We serve a God who is the eternally self-existent one. He is not the I was or the I will be. He is the I AM!

God has promised that He would forever be present with us. He said to the children of Israel:

"I AM the Lord that healeth thee" Exodus 15:26

God declares here that He is our healer, not He was our healer nor that He will be our healer.

He thunders to Moses and declares "I AM the Lord that heals you".

Whatever you are going through, just understand that you are only going through it. God has made a way for you to come through it.

Is it cancer? Is it HIV? Is it heart disease? Is it a lung disorder? Is it a neurological disorder? Is it a diabetic condition? Is it deafness? Is it depression? Is it addiction? Is it a sick child?

I don't know what it is that is keeping you up at night and causing you to lose sleep. I don't know what it is that has got you on the verge of surrender.

But I do know without a doubt that we serve a God who does not change.

"For I am the LORD, I change not" Malachi 3:6

He is still a miracle worker, He is still healer, He is still savior, and He is still deliverer!

"Jesus Christ the same yesterday, and today, and forever" Hebrews 13:8

Reach out to him in faith today. If He did it for one, he will do it for you.

As my Pastor and mentor Dr. Rod Parsley always so eloquently declares:

"The atmosphere of expectancy is the breeding ground of your miracle"

What are you expecting God to do for you?

Understand that Jesus already purchased your healing and deliverance almost 2000 years ago.

It is a done deal. All you need to do is appropriate it by faith in the finished work of the cross.

Your healing is more than a promise, it's a settled fact!

We serve a God of miracles!

Healing belongs to you.

It is your right.

It was purchased with the precious blood of the Lamb of God, the Prince of Glory, The Lord Jesus Christ.

I pray that as you read this book, faith would begin to come alive on the inside of you.

Faith to believe God for whatever you're in need of!

I desire for nothing less than the fullness of the revelation of God's will for you to be healed to break alive on the inside of you.

"If thou canst believe, ALL THINGS are POSSIBLE to him that believeth" Mark 9:23

About The Author

Chad MacDonald carries a powerful apostolic anointing that will change your life. He is the founder of Revival Fire World Ministries and also the International Director of Revival Fire International Bible Institute in Kisii, Kenya.

As an international revivalist and prophetic minister, Chad travels extensively both internationally and across America declaring the saving, healing and delivering power of Jesus Christ.

His meetings are marked with the tangible presence of God and accompanied by powerful signs and wonders. Chad's heart burns with the mandate of God to see true revival fire and the power of Pentecost ignited in the body of Christ.

For bookings or more information follow him on social media @revivalfirewm or on the web www.miraclerevivalfire.com